# STORIES OF MOTHER TERESA
## Her Smile and Her Words

*José Luis González-Balado*

**National Link of the
Co-Workers of Mother Teresa
in Spain**

*Translated by
Olimpia Diaz*

**LIGUORI**
PUBLICATIONS

One Liguori Drive
Liguori, Missouri 63057
(314) 464-2500

Imprimi Potest:
John F. Dowd, C.SS.R.
Provincial, St. Louis Province
Redemptorist Fathers

Imprimatur:
Monsignor Edward J. O'Donnell
Vicar General, Archdiocese of St. Louis

ISBN 0-89243-181-4
Library of Congress Catalog Card Number: 83-80948

This book has been adapted from the original Spanish version entitled *La Sonrisa de los Pobres,* published in Spain.

Cover design by Pam Hummelsheim

# A Word of Thanks

For their many hours of help in preparing the English-language edition of this book, the author would like to express deep thanks to two Co-Workers of Mother Teresa:

Janet Playfoot González, wife of the author and Co-Worker of Mother Teresa;

Eileen Egan, Consultant to the Co-Workers.

# About the Author

In Western Europe, books from the pen of José Luis González-Balado have been translated into French, Italian, Catalonian, Portuguese, German, and English. His writings include popular studies of Pope John Paul II, Brazilian archbishop Dom Helder Camara, Brother Roger of Taizé, and Ernesto Cardenal. The author's familiarity with Mother Teresa and her work flows from his involvement and leadership among Spain's Co-Workers of Mother Teresa.

# TABLE OF CONTENTS

## SHE EVOKES A RESPONSE . . .

## AND HER SMILE GOES ON
## REACHING OUT . . .

## BUT SHE DOESN'T ALWAYS SMILE

## APPENDIX

# Foreword

Mother Teresa — what an inspiration for a writer! Our first meeting was somewhat casual though intriguing, calling for renewed and deeper contact. The rarity of subsequent encounters has caused their details to be engraved upon my mind and has led to my seeking out those who have likewise experienced the profound human and spiritual impact of such personal encounters, with a view to sharing our blessings with others.

Having said this, I would assure the reader, however, that I have no intention of enlarging the image of this disarmingly simple woman beyond all human proportions. That would be a grave disservice to one whom I so respect.

Being a writer in quest of a personality with a story, meetings, such as my first with Mother Teresa, usually result in my finding a story and nothing more. But this was far different. It led to encounters through which a powerful contemporary beacon of Christianity was focused on the dark side of a lukewarm Christian's life. In what follows I remain indeed a newspaperman, but one who has undergone a profound transformation.

I have seen. I have heard. I've been impressed, and I'm moved to share what I've been a part of and what has become a part of me. The shock of the initial impact has been absorbed. Now I want to put my memories and the memories others have shared with me into words and to give witness, as

John did years after his experience of the Lord himself (1 John 1:3).

I have hopes that this book will not be "just another book about Mother Teresa and her work." I want, as far as possible, to share the experience of repeated personal encounters with her. In doing so, I do not intend, though I am aware of the danger of doing so, to reduce Mother Teresa's life to anecdote. Rather, I seek to reproduce the impact of repeated encounters with the living reality of her faith and love.

To enable the reader to go beyond anecdotes into their meaning, we have set Mother Teresa's own words into their context. Our hope is that deeds and words will authentically interpret each other.

I am fully aware that when a writer facilitates encounters with a person of such faith and love as Mother Teresa he unavoidably provides the occasion for some of his readers to consider for themselves that way of life, and I feel that I should address a few words specifically to such readers.

To begin with, it would perhaps be best to pass on what Mother Celine, who is responsible for aspirant formation of the Missionaries of Charity in Europe, confesses she has often told young women who came to her after reading such books as Malcolm Muggeridge's: "Well, now you have to forget what you have read and have to start living it."

When I visited two Spanish aspirants at the European house of formation of the Missionaries of Charity, both spoke with a serenity based on inner acceptance of their continuing experience, of how different the realities of their lives were from the romantic dreams that might prove superficially attractive to some. They spoke of a life marked by the severe demands of obedience and detachment — always present in every detail — a life that bases its free, generous, and lifelong surrender of self in service to the poorest of the poor upon a transforming consecration to God.

One thing became immediately clear in speaking to these aspirants: the Missionaries of Charity do everything in their power to remove the slightest romantic illusions from their recruitment and formation programs. Aspirants, without any exemptions or the slightest exception, are made to *experience* a way of life rigorously scheduled with long periods of contemplative prayer and hard work. And they are warned that this is no mere tough initiation but, rather, an introduction to a life that will be even harder!

And even then the clear vision of those responsible for the acceptance and formation of such candidates leads them to *dissuade* some who, they feel, are ill-suited to such a very hard life.

For my part, I hope, with the help of Father Chetcuti (see Appendix), to have realistically portrayed the spirit and life of the Missionaries of Charity, though fully aware that it is impossible to verbally capture the full spiritual reality.

May each person who reads this book have the courage to respond in his or her own unique way to what it suggests.

José Luis González-Balado

# HER SMILE
# REACHES OUT . . .

## to the suffering poor

At the home for the dying which the Missionaries of Charity have in Calcutta there was a man who had cancer, his body half-consumed by the sickness. Everyone had abandoned him as a hopeless case. Mother Teresa came near him to wash him tenderly. She encountered, at first, only the sick man's disdain.

"How can you stand my body's stench?" he asked.

Then, quite calmly the dying man said to her, "You're not from here. The people here don't behave the way you do."

Several minutes went by. And then the terminally ill man murmured a typical Indian expression: "Glory to you, woman."

"No," replied Mother Teresa. "Glory to you who suffer with Christ."

Then they smiled at each other. The sick man's suffering seemed to stop. He died two days later.

*Suffering by itself is nothing. But suffering as a share in Christ's Passion is a great gift. Man's greatest gift is the possibility of sharing Christ's Passion. Yes, it is a gift and a sign of God's love.*

*This is the way the Father showed his love for the world: giving us his Son to die for us. This is the way Christ showed that the greatest gift is love: he gave himself in suffering for us.*

Mother Teresa

## to those about to die

At the same house for the dying in Calcutta there is a small statue of Mary surrounded by small candles that are always lit. The statue is crowned with a gold tiara made from the rings of the women who died in that house. Each time Mother Teresa goes by the statue, as she takes a visitor around, she will say with evident emotion: "Those who had nothing have given a golden crown to the Mother of God!"

*Our Sisters, given to work in the midst of people who suffer unspeakable misery, are bravely facing many difficulties in numerous countries. But there is something truly beautiful in the people we work with: They are all so grateful and kind! It is enough to meet them. And to meet them, you just have to get near them.*

Mother Teresa

## to those who have given up

Mrs. Ann Blaikie, co-chairman of the International Association of Mother Teresa's Co-Workers, shares the following incident:

"One day as we were walking with Mother Teresa along the streets of Calcutta, a young man dashed up to us and knelt down to kiss Mother Teresa's feet. He told her that he was going to be married in a few hours. Mother Teresa explained to me that, a few months before, the young man had been brought, dying from hunger and tuberculosis, to the home for the dying. At the house he had been cared for and had learned a modest occupation, that of shining shoes. It had been enough to enable him to start a new life."

*Co-Workers should show a concrete kind of love. Our works of love are simply those of peace. Let us do them with even greater love and efficiency each person where he or she works, in his or her daily life, at home, with the neighbors.*

Mother Teresa

## to the "fallen away"

A zealous Irish priest, who had labored in vain for years to bring an estranged Catholic "back into the fold," shared the following story with me.

When Mother Teresa visited Ireland a prayer service was arranged in the local cathedral, with time set aside for Mother Teresa to address the crowd, and, of course, our priest's friend just had to be there! When her time came, Mother Teresa spoke simply of love for the poorest of the poor and of love for Christ through them.

Later on that night, after Mother Teresa had left

the city, the priest received a phone call from his "wayward" friend.

"Listen, I want to get back in the Church," said the man.

"What's happened?" asked the priest.

"Mother Teresa spoke to me," said the man.

"How could she have spoken to you? There were 5,000 people in the cathedral . . . ."

"I know, but her words were meant for me," replied the man.

The priest then asked, "And what did Mother Teresa say to you?"

"She said: *God bless you.*"

"I've said the same thing to you often, and I was never able to convince you . . . ."

"Yes, but Mother Teresa said it from the bottom of her heart," replied the man. And that is all the man could say to explain his decision to return to the Church.

*Be generous and understanding. Let no one come to you without feeling better and happier when they leave. Be the living expression of God's kindness: with kindness on your face, kindness in your eyes, kindness in your smile, kindness in your warm greeting.*

Mother Teresa

## to an unbeliever

When Mother Teresa started her work with the dying destitute she was in desperate need of a place in which to care for them. Local authorities in Calcutta offered her a section of the temple to the goddess Kali, which, though originally intended for the temporary housing of pilgrims, had become a hangout for thieves, drug addicts, and pimps. When the news circulated that the temple was being used by a woman and a foreigner and that she was trying ''to convert the poor to Christianity,'' groups of people protested at city hall. Others went to the nearest police station to demand that the woman be evicted. The police commissioner promised to do just that, but wanted first to personally check things out.

When the police commissioner went to see Mother Teresa, she was caring for a poor sick man by putting potassium permanganate on wounds from which worms were crawling out. The stench was unbearable.

Mother Teresa treated the officer with respect and offered to show him about. He answered that he preferred to look around on his own.

When he came out he met some of the people who had complained about Mother Teresa and said, ''I gave you my word that I would throw this woman out of here, and I would like to keep it. But, before I do so, you will have to get your mothers and sisters to do what she does. I make that the only condition for exercising my authority.''

*If anyone thinks and believes that the way he or she is taking is the only way toward God, that is the way God will take. If one knows no other way, if one has no doubts and does not feel the need to keep searching for another way, that is the way to salvation. That is the way God will take to reach that person.*

Mother Teresa

## to one without hope

The first person to bring Mother Teresa and her work to the attention of the Western World was the British newspaperman Malcolm Muggeridge. He began by filming a documentary for BBC television which was aired later by most European and American TV stations, and he went on to write a book which has gone through numerous printings and has been translated into twenty other languages, including those of several countries behind the Iron Curtain as well as some of those of Asia and Africa.

The public's response to Muggeridge's documentary and book was so immediate and pervasive that it gave evidence of her having touched even the hearts of those who could not bring themselves to admit it. Brother Andrew, cofounder with Mother Teresa of the Missionary Brothers of Charity, shared with me the following incident of which he learned from Mother Teresa herself.

Mother Teresa received a letter written by a man on the day of his intended suicide. He wrote that, on the preceding afternoon, he had worked out all the details for, what seemed to him, a perfectly "rational" suicide. And then, quite by accident, he came across Muggeridge's biography of Mother Teresa. Bored and with nothing else to do, he started to read it. As he read, he found that book, or rather that life, giving him a new interest in life, and, as he finished it, he moved back from the brink of suicide to begin life anew. The example of a woman, until then unknown to him, had given him hope.

*Let our lives give expression to the spirit of the Missionaries of Charity: total surrender to God with mutual trust and love for all. If we really receive this spirit, we will truly become Christ's co-workers — messengers of his love. This spirit should spring from your hearts and go out to your own families, neighborhoods, cities, countries, and to the whole world.*

Mother Teresa

## to a newly orphaned child

Abandoned children are of primary concern to the Missionaries of Charity. Mother Teresa's Sisters do all they possibly can to make orphaned and abandoned children happy, even though they know that there is no substitute for a real family. Mother Teresa tells the following anecdote: ''One day I discovered that a little one had lost his spark and his appetite after losing his mother. There was one Sister who looked like him, and the child would only smile and eat when he was near her. I entrusted the child to that Sister, after relieving her from her other duties for a few days. It did wonders for his health.''

*At times we can actually see happiness return to the lives of the dispossessed once they realize that many of us really care about them. And if they are sick, their health improves as well.*

Mother Teresa

## to one demanding trust

When Mother Teresa and the Missionaries of Charity are given money they receive it with gratitude because they know that money is a concrete sign of the love that people have for the poor — and the poor are the recipients of every last cent.

An eyewitness told me that he was present when a needy woman, or at least one who claimed to be needy, asked the Sisters for an amount equivalent to two hundred dollars. This amount was all the Sisters had. Without asking for any proof of her need, the Sisters immediately gave her the money, and the man went on to add, "Not long after that I saw a tall young man, a total stranger to myself and perhaps to the Sisters, knock on the Sisters' door and hand them some money. The amount turned out to be exactly two hundred dollars."

*We have to look for those who have no one. These are the victims of the worst illness: that of not being wanted, not being loved, that of not having any attention shown to them. We can find*

*Christ in them, Christ who is in the poor and the abandoned.*

Mother Teresa

## to a beggar with a mite

Mother Teresa herself tells of the day she met a beggar who gave her everything he had. "Everybody gives you something," he said, "and I'm going to also — in fact, everything I have."

"That day," Mother Teresa says, "the beggar had received but one bolivar (a small coin). He gave it to me and said: 'Take it, Mother Teresa, for your poor.' "

Mother Teresa adds, "In my heart I felt that the poor man had given me more than the Nobel Prize because he gave me all he had. In all probability, no one gave him anything else that night and he went to bed hungry."

*We have to be saints, not for the sake of being saints, but in order to offer Christ the opportunity to fully live in us. We have to be filled with love, faith, and purity, for the good of the poor whom we serve. Once we have learned how to look for God and his will, our contacts with the poor will serve to make saints of ourselves and others.*

Mother Teresa

## to a lonely, neglected man

One of the Co-Workers at a house of the Missionaries of Charity took a special liking for a certain very unhappy man. When the Co-Worker went on vacation for a few days he sent a postcard to his poor friend. Upon his return he discovered that the man had kept the postcard with great care and with good reason. "It was the first time in my entire life that the mail brought something addressed to me."

*Some people are known to us only by their address number. Do we really realize that such people exist? There could be a blind person across the street who would be happy if we offered to read the newspaper. Or even some rich person who has no one to visit him. He may be smothered by possessions and lack human contact that he really needs.*

Mother Teresa

## to the isolated elderly of Denmark

Mother Teresa carefully limits her use of the term "co-workers" to refer to those who actually share in her work with her.

There are today probably more than 150,000 such Co-Workers (people doing their best to discover and serve Christ in the poor). Some of them are Catholic; more of them are non-Catholic Christians; but the vast majority adhere to non-Christian religious traditions.

Among her Co-Workers in Denmark there is a group that knits sweaters and covers. It is made up of elderly men and women from all over Denmark who had been alone and sick. Now those who hardly knew their neighbors belong to a close-knit group of friends. Sick and elderly people who felt forgotten have united and found a reason for living. They are knitting in order to help poor children, and in doing so forget their own problems. They have been able to send 1,219 covers and 2,344 sweaters to Calcutta, Bombay, and Dacca.

*Diligence is the beginning of sanctity. If at the source of this were concern for others, we would become more and more like Christ whose heart was meek and humble and who acted out of concern for others. Our vocation derives its beauty precisely from our concern for others. Jesus spent his life doing good. In Cana Mary did nothing else but think of other's needs and make Jesus aware of them.*

Mother Teresa

## to an English priest

An English priest had decided to go to India to work in the slums among the poor, and so notified Mother Teresa. He expressed the desire to join the Missionary Brothers of Charity, who follow a rule of life similar and perhaps even more austere than that of the Sisters. Mother Teresa dissuaded him: "Don't do that, Father. Stay where you are and take care of the poor in your country. My poor are easy to take care of because they are satisfied with a piece of bread and a cloth to cover their bodies. That's why my work is easier than yours. The poor in your country are poor in spirit. That's why it is harder to get rid of their kind of poverty."

*We have to love those who are nearest to us, in our own family. Love will then go out to all who need us. We have to get to know the poor who are all around us; only then will we be able to understand them and love them. And only when we love them will we be able to serve them.*

Mother Teresa

## to a French priest

The Abbé Christian Daleau is grateful for the new and more authentic dimension that Mother Teresa brought to his priestly life. A busy "friend" of few words, he shared the following.

I was in Rome having just become the one in charge of the French Co-Workers. I told Mother Teresa that I was giving up my job as literature professor in order to give myself entirely to her work.

Her response was simple and clear: "Not for me, but for Jesus."

I simply cannot forget what Mother Teresa said to me twice: "Father, you think too much. Pray. If God wants what you are looking for, you will find a way to do it. Put everything in his hands."

*The more we are able to store up in our hearts through silent prayer, the more we will be able to give out in our work. We need silence in order to be able to touch people. The essential thing is not what we say but what God says to us and through us. All our words will be useless if they don't come from inside. Words that do not spread Christ's light add to the darkness.*

Mother Teresa

## to a Missionary Sister

From what could be the account of the opening of any of the many houses of the Missionaries of Charity, we've taken the following. It is from a letter written by the Superior of the most recent foundation in the United States.

"Mother Teresa stayed with us for three days. What a privilege to have her with us! She shared our work from morning till night, taking care of the hardest jobs and, at the same time, did not complain about all the people who wanted to see her and talk to her. Mother Teresa taught us, worked with us, and did for us what we could not do. For many of us it was the first time we were involved in starting a new place. We hope we will never forget those three days, especially her praying, her tenderness and kindness, and her love in action."

*We all long for heaven where God is, but we have the possibility of being in heaven right now, of being happy with God at this very moment. Being happy with God at this very moment means loving the way he loves, helping the way he helps, giving the way he gives, serving the way he serves, saving the way he saves. It means being with him twenty-four hours a day by touching him in those who suffer.*

Mother Teresa

## to a "living saint"

Jean Vanier, who knows Mother Teresa very well and who himself has been called a "living saint," writes:

"Each time I meet her she tells me about the suffering in Amman, Bangladesh, Lima. She tells me about the poverty in New York and Caracas. Talks about the lepers in Yemen, the anguish in Tanzania. She is obsessed by suffering, inequalities, divisions. But her obsession is one of love. She longs to be able to offer solutions, bread to the hungry, the Good News of Jesus to those without hope. Mother Teresa, just like Jesus, has a universal heart which has been hurt by the world's misery."

*The Christian has to learn to forgive. We have to realize that in order to be forgiven we have to be able to forgive. I am thinking about Northern Ireland, Bangladesh, Amman, and such places. Only if they succeed in forgiving will they find peace.*

Mother Teresa

## to the Pope

Paul Charron, a Canadian Co-Worker of Mother Teresa, was present when the Missionaries of Charity opened a small house in Detroit in June 1979. He shares with us the following brief and unadorned account of a conversation which she told him she had had with the Holy Father: "Bless me, Holy Father. Pray for me so I won't ruin God's work." "Of course, Mother. But you also pray for me so I won't ruin his Church . . . ."

*I don't think there is anyone else who needs God's help and grace more than I do. I feel so forsaken and confused at times! And I think that's exactly why God uses me: because I cannot claim any credit for what gets done. On the contrary, I need his help twenty-four hours a day. And if days were longer, I would need even more of it.*

Mother Teresa

## to a non-Catholic coordinator

Jan Colenbrander is the coordinator of Mother Teresa's Dutch Co-Workers. He recalls the very first time she spoke to him.

"I told her I belonged to the Dutch Reformed Church (Protestant) and that I just couldn't see myself becoming a Catholic. Among other things, I told her that I was bothered by the pope and the Virgin Mary. She answered me, 'We would not have Jesus if it weren't for Mary.' Later, she wrote to me, 'Love for Our Lady keeps growing in your heart. Keep Jesus' joy in your heart as your strength, so that one day you will come to love her like Jesus loved her. Then she,

27

who is the cause of our joy for having given us Jesus, will become your joy too.' "

Jan Colenbrander added, "Understanding is growing. I pray for unity."

*Love prayer. Let yourself become aware of the need for prayer often during the day. And do it! Prayer makes the heart grow until it is able to contain God himself. Ask and seek, and your heart will become large enough to include Christ and to keep him inside.*

Mother Teresa

## to those across language barriers

Mother Teresa does not know many languages, but when it comes to communicating she is an expert.

Her most eloquent way of communicating is through her smile. Mother Teresa and her Sisters are all blessed with this seal of their profound happiness. Their spontaneous, frequent, and natural smiles spring from their enjoyment of the simple things of life.

******

Mother Teresa is very frequently asked for her autograph. But she never stops at just her signature if she has time. For those she knows better, she writes something personal, very fitting, encouraging, at once spiritual and intimate.

No matter how busy she is, she always ends her letters and talks with, God bless you! One day I asked her to write that phrase, "God bless you!" in Spanish for her Spanish-speaking Co-Workers: *Que Dios os bendiga*. I wrote it for her first, and she tried to copy it. She did it three times because she had made mistakes. The third time, she wrote *Bendiga* with a capital "B," and I was tempted to ask her to write the phrase a fourth time using a lower case "b." But I didn't because I thought that perhaps it was intentional — Mother Teresa always writes another word with a capital letter: Poor.

# AND THE SMILE GOES ON

A novice who could not master English was working in London, in a house for the abandoned elderly. One of the old men in the house had taken a liking to the Spanish novice. She was in charge of taking care of him, and the liking was mutual. But the old man did not know Spanish.

"He talks and talks when I am with him. I don't know what he is saying. I imagine he is telling me about his life. I also talk to him, even though I don't think he understands my Spanish. I am having a very hard time with English. But we smile a lot. We communicate very well through our smiles," said the novice.

*I am more and more convinced that the worst sickness there is for a human being is the lack of affection. Medicines have been discovered to cure leprosy and tuberculosis. But unless there are hands that are willing to serve and hearts available to love, this lack of affection is incurable.*

Mother Teresa

## to her very own and to the world

Many wonder how Mother Teresa reacted when she first heard that she had been awarded the Nobel Peace Prize. One of the Sisters who was with her when she found out gives the following account.

"On October 17, the news arrived that Mother Teresa had been awarded the 1979 Nobel Peace Prize. There was great joy among the Sisters in the community, but Mother Teresa's first reaction was to quietly go to the chapel to humbly pray and thank God for his gift to the poor. One by one, the rest of the Sisters followed her into the chapel and in unison sang a hymn of praise and thanksgiving to God. When we saw the number of television cameras, newspaper reporters, and people — including our poor — who came to congratulate her, we prayed even more for her. We asked God to help her, since it had been his will for her to give her all this, and to give her strength and health to endure it calmly and without weakening."

Her trip to Oslo was a very festive occasion for many, but not so much so for Mother Teresa. She wanted to share, symbolically, what the Nobel Prize meant to her with all her Sisters, and chose to do so through the first two who went with her when she left the Sisters of Loreto to start a new life. A few days before the date set for receiving the prize, Mother Teresa wrote the following: "God willing, on December 8th I will be in Oslo. Since the Nobel Prize committee has sent two tickets, besides my own, I will use them to show my love and gratitude for all the other Sisters in that first group who had the courage to go when there was nothing. Their joy was in having nothing and yet having Jesus to the fullest — in loving

Jesus they loved the poor. For all this I will be taking Sisters Agnes and Gertrude with me to Oslo.''

*The Nobel Prize has been given to me because of the poor. But I think that this prize goes beyond the obvious. It has, for a fact, awakened many consciences throughout the world. It has served as a reminder that the poor are our brothers and sisters and that we should give them proofs of our love for them. . . .*

*I never consider myself a person of importance because I have received a prize. It is more a case of Christ using me as his instrument to unite all those who are here. That's what I see happening: people drawn together to meet each other by their need of God. What I am most pleased with is the religious atmosphere that is created at such happenings. Everyone talks about God. This is a very beautiful experience for me. I think that my being able to get these people together so they can talk about God is a very wonderful thing. It is like a new hope for the world.*

Mother Teresa

# SOME SHE
# KEEPS WAITING . . .

---

In general, considerateness leads Mother Teresa to be on time for all appointments, no matter who is involved. The following incident proves the exception.

A friend and Mother Teresa had an appointment with the Apostolic Nuncio, and they were headed toward a punctual arrival. But, on the way to the nunciature, they drove through a really poor section where the poorest of the poor lived, and Mother Teresa asked to stop and visit.

There among the poor she found a very old and absolutely destitute man. As she took care of him, washing him and cleaning his house, Mother Teresa lost track of time. The driver became impatient, and Mother Teresa arrived very late for her appointment with the Nuncio. Only a very poor person could have made Mother Teresa so late for an appointment. For her, the poor occupy the top place in the social hierarchy.

*We are touching Christ's body when we touch the poor. In them and through them, we feed the hungry Christ. It is the naked Christ whom we dress. It is the homeless Christ whom we take in. It isn't merely a case of being hungry for bread or lacking clothes or a roof for shelter. Christ is hungry today in the poor, but the rich are also hungry for love, care, for someone close to them.*

Mother Teresa

# SHE EVOKES
# A RESPONSE . . .

## from her admirers

I have heard people compare Mother Teresa with some more or less contemporary religious figures. In most cases, whoever was making the comparison did not seem very convinced of it and would say that Mother Teresa only resembled *herself*. I have heard comparisons made with Dom Helder Camara, Martin Luther King, Charles de Foucauld — and, in some instances, comparisons were made with some officially recognized and approved saints. She has been compared to Saint Teresa, even though Mother Teresa herself says that, in spite of the name, she takes her inspiration from the Little Flower, not from Saint Teresa of Avila. The French insist on comparing her with a great French saint: Saint Vincent de Paul, the apostle of charity.

But it was not always so.

When Mother Teresa visited Spain for the first time, on June 2, 1976, it took some time to convince the chief of police to allow her into the country.

When finally told that everything was fine, she revealed that she also had a second passport: a diplomatic one issued to her by the Vatican State.

Paul VI had personally offered it to her. He was a great admirer of her and a benefactor in her work. He had given this passport to her to facilitate her entry into Bangladesh when her Indian passport would have hindered her mission of "universal love."

When she returned to Spain in 1980 after winning the 1979 Nobel Peace Prize the police were very kind to her. She had to wait, however, for her luggage, just like the other passengers, for over an hour.

Finally, when the attendant at the luggage carrousel spotted Mother Teresa's cardboard box tied with a string, in the middle of the better-looking luggage of the other passengers, he quickly grabbed it, gave it to her, kissed her hand, and said: "Mother, you deserve this and much more."

In the meantime, others had recognized her. A group of Japanese people asked her to pose with them for a picture, and Mother Teresa did so. An American girl asked her for her autograph, and Mother Teresa did not refuse her. The young girl, lacking a piece of paper, offered her a page of her passport.

There were quite a number of people waiting for passengers, but there was a small number waiting for Mother Teresa. When the crowd saw her and recognized her, a round of applause was offered in her honor. Mother Teresa simply smiled at everyone and greeted them with an Indian greeting: both hands joined above her head.

Immediately upon arrival at the Sisters' house, Mother Teresa asked to see the chapel. She liked it very much and asked the two priests, who had been sent by the Cardinal-Archbishop of Madrid to welcome her, if there could be a Mass celebrated right away, even before she saw the rest of the house.

After Mass she was offered dinner, and she wanted everybody to eat with her. She ate very little but was not ungrateful. She took a piece of bread, an orange, and a glass of water. She also ate a piece of cheese that she had saved from the plane. She encouraged the others to eat more, but for the moment they seemed to imitate her.

*Let us become real branches, filled with fruit, on Jesus' vine. Let us welcome him into our lives whenever he wants to come in. He comes as Truth which must be spoken, as Life which must be lived, as Light which must be reflected, as Love which must be loved, as the Way which we must take, as Happiness which we must spread, as Peace which we must plant, as Sacrifice which we must offer in our families, and with our neighbors — whether near or far.*

Mother Teresa

## from her daughters

In June 1980 when Mother Teresa was to welcome four of the Sisters to the first home in Spain all scheduling broke down, to the consternation of her Co-Workers; but, in doing so, there was revealed the unique life-style of Mother Teresa and her daughters.

The four Sisters arrived in Barcelona on time, but the only seats on the train that would have brought them on to Madrid according to schedule were reserved for passengers ticketed at a higher fare, and the poor Sisters simply did not have the necessary cash. When offered plane fare to Madrid the Sisters were grateful for the offer, but found it not in keeping with their identification with the poor. They accepted food and coffee and waited for the morning train. When Mother Teresa arrived she was told that the Sisters would not arrive at 8:00 P.M. but rather at 8:00 A.M. the next morning. Her evident and immediate concern for their safety revealed her great motherly love for them, but when assured that the four Sisters were fine and had merely missed the train because of lack of funds Mother Teresa said quite calmly, "It's better that way. I travel by plane in order to save time because I have to go to so many places. The Sisters are better off traveling by train."

The next morning, Mother Teresa asked to be awakened at 5:00 A.M. and personally went to meet her daughters at the train station when they arrived.

*We have to make greater efforts so that each Sister and Brother, as well as each Co-Worker, grows in his or her likeness to Christ so that Christ may live his life of kindness in today's world. Your love for Christ has to be great. Keep Christ's light shining in your hearts always be-*

*cause he is our only way. He is the life we have to live. He is the love we have to love.*

Mother Teresa

## from the desperate destitute

After having combed the streets of Calcutta in search of the poor, Mother Teresa and the two who relate the incident found a small boy who looked more foreign than Indian at the door of the motherhouse. He had a sign around his neck which said, ''Mother Teresa, thanks for taking me in!''

The same two people shared with me an even more unbelievable experience. A few hours before they found the boy, the two of them had helped Mother Teresa to take a newborn from a dog's mouth. Someone had abandoned the baby in a garbage pile. Unfortunately, the baby, though alive when found, did not survive for long.

*Christ has said that we are more important in his Father's eyes than the grass, the birds, and the flowers in the fields. Therefore, if he takes care of these things, he will take much better care of his life in us. He means what he says. Life is God's greatest gift to human beings who, understandably, are of such concern to him since they are made in his image. We don't have any right to destroy it.*

Mother Teresa

# from those who share her experience

Mother Teresa often repeats that the poor are "wonderful and kind." Brother Andrew, the co-founder of the Missionary Brothers of Charity, says that he is convinced that Mother Teresa says this so often because there is a danger of our having a paternalistic and condescending attitude toward the poor, to whom we consider ourselves superior. "This attitude is without foundation. The poor are great people. Very often they have to lead heroic lives. They are gifted with great generosity, love, and tenderness. Their courage and strength of character in the face of life's hardships confirm the fact of their heroism. The kindness, the smiles, and tenderness they so often show us should lead us to feel humble in their presence."

Among those who regularly help the Missionaries of Charity in their soup kitchen on Huertas Street in Madrid is José Luis Hipola.

He feels that this work has not so much meant a change of attitude as of opportunity. He hadn't known how to get close to the poor except through giving money at times to beggars. But now José Luis says, "The Sisters have built a bridge between the poor and us."

And he goes on to say, "Having contact with the poor who come to *Estrella de la Mañana* has led me to discover in them people with great values — a sense of friendship, of dignity, of self-esteem. They also have a superior sense of humor. They can take a joke and joke with others, in spite of the fact that in many instances their situation is humanly unbearable. Many of the poor lack only one thing: the ability to earn money.''

*The poor, the lepers, the dispossessed, the neglected, and even the alcoholics we serve are all great people. Many of them have extraordinary personalities. We should communicate the experience that comes from serving them to those who have never had the opportunity. It is one of the greatest comforts in our work.*

Mother Teresa

## from her Co-Workers throughout the world

Mother Teresa does not ask for great monetary contributions from her Co-Workers. This is evident in her own words: ''Don't worry so much about results and numbers. Every act of love toward a poor or marginal person, small though it be, is important in Jesus' eyes.''

Some American Co-Workers wrote, ''We are few in number. We are forming a prayer and work group. Our activities are as different as we all are. A Co-Worker who is a nurse has taken on as her mission of love the care of seriously ill cancer patients. Others give copies of Mother Teresa's biography to friends and acquaintances so they will become enthusiastic about her work. There are some who, during the Christmas season, give no other gifts but this biography. One Co-Worker visits the patients who are in a mental hospital near his home. And there are some who visit and offer companionship and help to those who are sick or elderly in the slums and have no one else.''

A young engaged French couple wrote: ''We will be married in a month. We have asked our relatives and friends that instead of getting gifts for us, they give the amount they would have spent to Mother Teresa's poor. We want to have a small intimate wedding without uselessly spending money.''

The woman in charge of our Paris Co-Workers asked me to be an interpreter so she could ask Mother Teresa a question. ''What is the most important thing for the Co-Workers?''

Mother Teresa looked at her with a big smile on her lips and said: ''To be holy!''

*Love should be in season all year long and within the reach of everyone. Everyone can harvest love without limit. Everyone can obtain this love through meditation, a spirit of prayer and sacrifice, through an intense inner life.*

Mother Teresa

# from her ''French-speaking friends''

In France, since World War II, the word ''co-workers'' carries connotations of collaboration with the enemy. Consequently, French and French-speaking supporters of Mother Teresa in Canada, Belgium, Luxembourg, and Switzerland are called *amis* — friends.

From among the many incidents which could be recounted to illustrate the response of these "friends" to Mother Teresa, I have chosen two.

"I am sending a check for a small amount. I had decided to buy myself a coat for this winter, but after thinking it over I have decided that the one I have will last for a couple more years. The check is for the amount I would have spent on the coat, which can wait."

The second concerns a telephone operator: "I am sending a money order for 525 francs. This amount is more or less what I would spend on my evening meals for a month. I am giving up my evening meals at the boardinghouse where I live. I thought that someone like myself, who, thank God, is in very good health, can give up a meal to help those who are hungry. I have decided to send the exact amount every month."

*Our work is nothing more than the expression of the love we have for God. We have to pour this love out on someone. Through people we express our love for God.*

*Love has to be based on sacrifice. We have to give until it hurts.*

Mother Teresa

## from captivated American throngs

Rochester, Minnesota, is one of the "bases" of Mother Teresa's American Co-Workers. After a prayer meeting held in the cathedral there on July 21, 1976, Mother Teresa was subjected to an enthusiastic but exhausting press conference.

She was asked how the Missionaries of Charity spend their busy days, how they were able to live and work in such places as the South Bronx and in countries like India where Catholics are in the small minority.

Each long and thoughtful answer that Mother Teresa gave was received with loud and long-lasting applause. And there came a time when the people applauded before an answer was given, to express their feelings for the question or, better still, the plea that was heard coming from among those present.

Then someone asked Mother Teresa, who was standing behind the microphone, to take a few steps forward so that "we'll be able to see such a beautiful woman." Mother Teresa, somewhat confused, had no other choice but to take a few steps toward the middle of the room. And with a very humble smile on her lips said, "Not a beautiful woman, but a beautiful sari!" And the applause was deafening.

******

In Oslo, on the occasion of the awarding of the Nobel Prize, speaking with some national Co-Workers, Mother Teresa told them that some Americans had said to her: "Mother, it seems they want to canonize you."

She responded, *"Let me die first."*

*Since each Missionary of Charity should be Christ's co-worker in the slums, she has to understand what God and the Congregation expect of her. Christ should be able to live his life and to radiate through her in the slums. When the poor see her work, they should feel attracted to Christ and invite him to come into their homes and their lives. The sick and the suffering should be able to find an angel of mercy and tenderness in her. The children of the streets should hold on to her arm, seeing in her a reflection of Christ, the friend of the little ones.*

Mother Teresa

## from first communicants

A catechist in a parish sent a gift to a center of Mother Teresa's Co-Workers. The meaning of the gift is apparent in the explanation which accompanied it: "This gift comes from the children of the 3rd grade in EGB (school) who are getting ready to make their First Communion. They all gladly gave up the gifts they would have received to make it possible. They have assured me that *having contributed to saving a life* would add more to this solemn occasion than any material gift. They want to share their happiness with some young friends in India."

*Our lepers, our paralytics, our unwanted, and our unloved — they all need love and kindness and to be treated like human beings. In the Sacred Host, during Mass, we see and we touch Christ's body. We should treat Christ's body in the poor with the same tenderness and love, and with the same faith.*

Mother Teresa

# from children in Austria

Children, free from the skepticism which often characterizes adults, are sensitive to Mother Teresa's work and life-style. A group of Austrian children, after deciding to become her Co-Workers, wrote to her about their decision.

"Dear Mother Teresa: A few days ago we heard about you in our religion class. We were shown some slides which showed the misery of the people in Calcutta and what you are doing for them. We were very impressed by your love for these people. You worry about those who don't have a home and take care of the dying, giving them hope and strengthening their faith.

"You have shown us that riches don't make us happy, but that God's love, the love of his Son Jesus, and the love of those around us do. You give us a great example, and we want to do all we can to imitate you and offer you our help. We want to build God's kingdom right here and now.

"We are sending a small contribution to show you that we admire your work. We wish you and all your Co-Workers the needed strength to serve others and a lot of patience and happiness. We pray for you and ask God's abundant blessings on you. And we are sure you will receive them since Jesus said: Blessed are the merciful, because mercy will be shown to them."

*We come across Jesus himself in the poor, the same Christ that Saint Paul met on his way to Damascus. Saul was on his way to kill, to exter-*

*minate Christians. Jesus asked him: "Saul, Saul,*
*why do you persecute me?" Saul asked in turn:*
*"Who are you, Lord?" "I am Jesus whom you*
*are persecuting," was Christ's reply.*

Mother Teresa

## from children throughout the world

From the beginning, children have responded
to her smile and shared in Mother Teresa's work.

In Spain, every week children in public as well
as private schools share the money they receive
for snacks and entertainment with Mother Teresa's poor.

A Japanese woman writes: "My eight-year-old
son has come up with an idea that we have all
accepted: to give up dessert three times a week to
help the poor children in India."

The children of France have tried, over the
years, to help defray the ever-increasing costs of
Mother Teresa's travels. In this, they have
received help from some airline companies which
offer her free tickets to wherever she happens to
be going.

For over ten years, the school children of Denmark have been sending shipments of powdered
milk and vitamin pills. These children were concerned and wanted to help their poor friends in
India. Each monthly shipment consists of 320
boxes of milk and 200,000 vitamin pills.

A group of school children in Canada did
something uniquely moving: They went on sev-

eral twenty-four-hour fasts to experience what the children in India suffer. Their program was called *a ton of hunger,* and consisted of acquiring and sending a ton of food stuff to the children of India. They were able to purchase and send the shipment through their voluntary fasts.

*All life is God's life in us. Even an unborn child has God's life in him or her. We have no right whatsoever to destroy such a life, whatever ways there might be of doing so. Man, woman, or child — there is no difference. It seems to me that a cry from those unborn children is reaching us, children who are being murdered before coming into this world — a cry that echoes and reechoes before God's throne.*

*Many people find it hard to care for the unborn and that is why they try to get rid of them. They even go to the extreme of getting rid of their unborn children by ending their lives. This is a terrifying symptom even in a very poor country, but especially in a country where it represents a freely chosen position of the people. What I believe is that no human hand should be raised to end life.*

Mother Teresa

## from those in positions of power and influence

After receiving the Nobel Peace Prize in 1979 Mother Teresa was to receive further recognition — including the Bharat of India.

In July 1980, when the President of Venezuela decided to award the *Orden del Libertador* (Order of the Liberator) to Mother Teresa, on the 15th anniversary of the founding of the Missionaries of Charity in Venezuela, problems were foreseen in getting her to Caracas on time, so she was flown in the presidential plane by its crew. The jet left Caracas and was back in no time. On board, along with a complete crew, were only two passengers: Mother Teresa, confused because of all the honor bestowed on her and, yet, detached from all humanly bestowed honor, and Sister Dolores, the pioneer of the Missionaries of Charity in Venezuela.

The presidential interpreter, a non-Catholic who had served as interpreter to many presidents and many famous men and women, confessed that he experienced his biggest thrill in translating the words of this real saint.

Mother Teresa was awarded the *Orden del Libertador* at the *Casona,* the presidential palace in Venezuela. In giving the award, President Luis Herrera Campins stated that it was ''a symbolic acknowledgment of the universal work of Mother Teresa for the poor — a work not just for the poor but for the poorest of the poor.'' An eyewitness observed Mother Teresa, almost immediately, put the medal into the little cloth bag Missionaries of Charity carry and noted that sometimes, after receiving awards, Mother Teresa has been known to leave without them. (Whatever awards she has kept she does not exhibit.)

The awarding of the prize in Caracas was to be followed by a banquet at the *Casona*. Mother Teresa was to be the honored guest along with her companions, but she declined this honor and returned to the Sisters' house in Catia la Mar where she had a meal just like the one the poor in the neighborhood were having.

*We are merely instruments who do our small part and disappear.*

Mother Teresa

## from two royal women

When, in the early 1970s, Mother Teresa had occasion to meet King Balduino of Belgium, the king asked her to go to the hospital with him to visit Queen Fabiola who was quite sick. She had expressed the desire to meet and talk to Mother Teresa. Mother Teresa accepted gladly.

Upon meeting her, the queen asked Mother Teresa to pray for her; and Mother Teresa, the queen, and King Balduino began to recite the rosary right then and there. When Mother Teresa left the hospital she expressed admiration for the simple faith of the king and queen.

At a later date, word was brought to Mother Teresa at a press conference in Madrid that Queen Sofía wanted to see her and talk to her. Would Mother Teresa wait for a half hour?

Mother Teresa waited and Doña Sofía arrived on time. Her going over to see Mother Teresa was doubly noteworthy: It was King Juan Carlos' feast day and Doña Sofía took time out while an official ceremony was taking place at the palace.

Doña Sofía expressed her regret that the king was prevented by another commitment from seeing her and talking to her personally. At the press conference Mother Teresa had just said that she would have liked to share the Nobel Peace Prize with Don Juan Carlos.

*When Jesus talks about hunger he not only refers to physical hunger but to a hunger for love, for understanding, for warmth. He certainly experienced a lack of affection — he came among his own and was rejected. He knew the meaning of loneliness, rejection, and of "belonging nowhere." This kind of hunger is very prevalent in our world today; and it is destroying many lives, many homes, and many countries. Being dispossessed refers not only to not having a roof over our head but also to not having someone who understands us and is kind to us. This kind of deprivation cries out for someone to open up his or her heart and to take in the lonely, who have no family or human affection of any kind.*

Mother Teresa

## from an American Senator

Senator Edward Kennedy visited Calcutta in 1971, at a time when millions of refugees from Bangladesh were pouring into India. On his visit he met Sister Agnes who was cleaning a ward for cholera patients. Kennedy came up to her to shake her hand, and Sister Agnes warned him that her hands were dirty. Kennedy told her, ''The dirtier they are the more honored I will feel.''

*The poor! They are the people we have to meet. They are Jesus yesterday, today, and tomorrow, and both you and I have to meet them. Once we know them, we will love them, and love will make us offer them our help. Let's not be content with merely offering them money or material things. Money isn't everything, nor is it the hardest thing to get. The poor need hands that serve them and hearts that love them. Christianity is love. It means spreading love all around us.*

Mother Teresa

## from a consular official

In the mid-seventies, Mother Teresa was told of Haiti's extreme poverty, and she was easily convinced of how good it would be to open up a house there for the Missionaries of Charity. When she mentioned her intention of flying there from Venezuela, two friends, one a citizen of Venezuela, drove her to the consul's office and, leaving her in their VW, tried to take care of her visa application for her.

The consul refused them outright, ''No, even a twenty-four-hour visa is not possible.''

''But you don't understand. This visa is for someone who has no political ties whatsoever. Her only motive is humanitarian.''

"I said it was not possible! Everybody has left the office by now. It can't be done. But . . . you said this was a nun. What kind of a nun?"

Then they had a chance to tell him about this extraordinary nun, whose only concern was for the poor, and of the awards she had received; and the consul asked to see her in person.

When they met, Mother Teresa smiled and greeted the consul in the Indian fashion — hands joined above her head. She said, even before he could speak: "Thanks! Thanks!"

Things changed radically because of her greeting and her words of thanks — or perhaps because of her smile. The consul said to her: "Mother, I am going to give you a visa right away. And not for just twenty-four hours but for a whole year, and would you happen to have a wallet-sized picture of yourself?"

Mother Teresa, one of the most photographed people in the world, never carries any pictures of herself and, of course, had none with her. But the consul persisted, "It doesn't matter, Mother, I will still give you the visa. But, please, would you send me a large picture of yourself so I can have it here in my office?"

Mother Teresa's companions took care of the matter for him.

*It isn't necessary to go out to the slums to find a lack of love and poverty. There is someone who suffers in every family and in every neighborhood.*

Mother Teresa

## from Communists
## and other politicians

The news of the Nobel Prize prompted the Communist prime minister of Bengal, Jyoti Basu, to give a reception in Mother Teresa's honor. "Up to this point you have been Bengal's mother," Jyoti Basu said to Mother Teresa. "Now you have become the mother of the entire world."

When President Varahagiri Venkata Giri awarded Mother Teresa the Nehru Prize for International Understanding in 1972, he said: "Mother Teresa is one of those superior souls who have gone beyond all barriers of race, religion, creed, and nationality."

There is something which goes beyond religious, ethical, and racial categories; even political ones. When Mother Teresa went to vote during local Indian elections, a member of one of the Bengal political parties said to her, "Mother Teresa, you should not vote. You should not give your vote to any party. You belong to everyone."

*Sharing love with the poor makes us closer to one another as well as to the poor. And this leads to our knowing the poor better. Knowledge leads us to love and sacrifice: to personally serve our neighbors. That's why I heartily invite all of you, without excluding anyone — rich, young, and adults — to place yourselves at the service of Christ in the poor, to give your hearts in love to Christ in them.*

Mother Teresa

# from a TV host in Spain

Spanish television devoted a long program to Mother Teresa on July 21, 1980. Friends present at the taping heard one of the crew say, "I've never seen Joaquín Soler Serrano more impressed with anyone." Mother Teresa sat down with an air of serenity and then, facing the interviewer, adjusted the headset and made the sign of the cross. Throughout the entire interview she never let go of the rosary she had in her hands.

She answered all questions except those of a personal nature. The personal ones she avoided by courteously saying: *Let's not talk about that; it isn't important. Let us talk about our people.* (By which, of course, she meant the poor.)

At the end of the interview, Soler Serrano asked Mother Teresa if there was a message she wanted to communicate to the people of Spain. Mother Teresa was very brief: "Pray!" Her host was a bit startled; he seemed to have thought there would be a longer response. The cameras were still on Mother Teresa, and the microphones were still on. Mother Teresa stood up and ended the interview. She said: "So, let's pray!"

When asked to pose for a group picture, Mother Teresa agreed and, while everyone was getting ready, following her own advice led the director, his secretary, the technicians, and those standing around in the Our Father.

*We don't have to do great things to show great love for God and neighbor. It is the love we put into our actions which makes our offering some-thing beautiful for God.*

Mother Teresa

## from a French interviewer

An interviewer for a French periodical expressed his personal reaction thus:

"Mother Teresa has no other obsession than to discover among the poorest of the poor Christ's hurt, buffeted, disfigured, and battered face and to adore it in its agony. This face is seen in the thousands along the muddy, fetid, and infected streets of Calcutta. The houses of the Missionaries of Charity take in every kind of human discard — the tubercular, the sick, the lepers — abandoned by mankind but loved by God. Jesus did the very same thing twenty centuries ago in Palestine. *The gospel is not dead.*"

*Christ is present today in the people who are considered unwanted, who have no job, who do not receive any attention or care, who are hungry, who have no clothing or shelter. The state and society consider them parasites. No one has time for them. You and I are worthy, as Christians, of Christ's love if our love is real. We have the duty of searching out such people and helping them. They are there so we can go to meet them.*

Mother Teresa

## from postal workers everywhere

Mother Teresa's motherly love for her daughters is evident. The Missionaries of Charity profess the same filial devotion for Mother Teresa. However, when the time comes for detachment, for accepting a mission that takes the daughters away from their mother, they all accept the sacrifice willingly.

Though Mother Teresa does her best to guide, stimulate, and comfort them by her letters, that is often impossible, even though she finds herself writing late into the night after long hours spent in the service of the poor.

When she was about to leave Spain after the first house of the Missionaries of Charity was opened there in Madrid, Mother Teresa asked the author for the exact address of the new place. I replied that I had never paid attention to the street number but that I had heard the name *Barrio del Candil*, but I had also read that the area was called *Vereda de los Estudiantes*. I assured her, however, that once the Sisters moved in there would be no need for detail because they would make the area very popular. Mother Teresa smiled and said quite simply: "I get letters which merely say: Mother Teresa, India."

*If we were able to see God's image in our neighbor, do you think weapons and generals would be needed?*

*It would amount to a real explosion of God's love here on earth if we were merely to clothe the naked Christ through our charitable words and by protecting the good name of others.*

Mother Teresa

## from a travel agent

A Spanish travel agent shared the following experience with the author. In June 1980, in an exquisite little pastry shop in the center of Madrid, he overheard one girl mention to another that she had read in the paper that Mother Teresa was staying at the time in Leganés, on the outskirts of Madrid. When he heard the news, having seen her work in India, he forgot about the pastry he had come for and headed for Leganés. There, in Leganés, he was surprised by the absolute simplicity of it all. There he saw the Nobel Peace Prize winner hanging out the clothes to dry and explaining to her daughters that the ropes had to be taut and at a certain height in order to avoid the shade from the roof.

Later, Mother Teresa explained to the Sisters what kind of simple cabinets they needed to keep their clothes, and the young man offered to bring some wood the next day and to build them.

Later in the day, when all attempts on the part of the community to get Mother Teresa a critically important flight to Yugoslavia had been to no avail, the young man came up to her and said, "Mother, tomorrow at 9:15 in the morning your problem will be solved. I will take care of it at my office because I work for a travel agency."

At this, someone remarked to Mother Teresa,

"Mother, isn't there an English expression that says 'the right man at the right moment'?" Mother Teresa replied: "It always happens that way. We are thinking about solving a problem; and, before we find the solution, someone we don't know comes into the picture, someone we hadn't thought about, and we have the solution."

Later that day, when Mother Teresa had to go to the parish church in Leganés, the same Pascual Cervera had the privilege of taking her there in his Mini-Austin. As he drove, he felt impelled to confide in Mother Teresa. He told her about his desire to serve others and how he just couldn't think of concrete ways of doing it. Mother Teresa explained that one way to do it was to do one's work well. She told him that the important thing was love, that if he did his work with love, God would turn his work into service. "I'm sure that sometimes," Mother Teresa told him, "you have to have a lot of patience with your clients, isn't that true?" Pascual answered, "Yes, that's true." "Well, do your job patiently and lovingly, and you will be serving others. And then pray. Don't ever stop praying, Pascual," Mother Teresa said.

Pascual says that Mother Teresa was right. He has found new meaning in his work. He says that ever since that day he has reflected about a prevalent attitude among people who work for the public: They show a rather obvious hostility, as if taking care of people were humiliating. He says that this attitude would be eliminated by listening to Mother Teresa's advice — put love into the work you do.

When Pascual was parking the car by the church, Mother Teresa pointed to a poor man who was begging by the door and said, "Pascual, there's one of mine." There were a lot of people waiting for her, but Mother Teresa was talking about the poor man. She headed straight for him and started talking to him, telling him about the money he had in his hat which was on the ground. The poor man probably did not understand her words, but he seemed impressed, even though he didn't know this was a very important woman. Mother Teresa saw that one of his hands was deformed by rheumatism or arthritis. It was dirty, too, and the man was trying to hide it. Mother Teresa reached down and caressed it several times lovingly and went inside the church.

*Let us not live unaware. Let us, rather, look for our own way of being able to understand our brothers and sisters. If we would like to better understand those with whom we live, we have to be able to understand ourselves first.*

Mother Teresa

## from an American contractor

When Mother Teresa opened the first American house of the Missionaries of Charity in Harlem, one of her first visitors, checkbook in hand, offered to give the Sisters whatever money they could possibly need. Mother Teresa said to him, "Thank you, but we don't need any money. What we need is land — a lawn — a yard."

There was a big lot available but full of rubbish.

The Sisters wanted to turn it into a park that all the people in that overpopulated and unhealthy area could enjoy.

The man with the checkbook answered: "I'm in the construction business. I have tractors and trucks. They're at your service with enough men to operate them." The building of the public park took only a few days.

Such responses to Mother Teresa's needs are not rare.

*I would like it very much if our Co-Workers, each in his or her own immediate environment, would concentrate more and more on giving service freely and generously to the poor. Let each of them seek out those who live alone, who lack affection, those cut off, in any way, and try to see in them the suffering Christ.*

*Give someone a smile, visit someone for a short time, make a fire for someone who is cold, read something to someone. These are small things, very small, but they will make your love for God more concrete.*

*Money is useful only if it serves to spread Christ's love. It can serve to feed the hungry Christ. But he is hungry not just for bread, but for love, for your presence, for your human contact.*

*To offer a home to the homeless Christ, start by making our own homes places where peace, happiness, and love abound, through your love for each member of your family and for your neighbors.*

Mother Teresa

# from an adolescent in Brazil

The following letter speaks for itself.

"I am fifteen years old. I have just finished reading the biography of Mother Teresa of Calcutta and am filled with admiration for her work.

"Though far from gullible, I believe your book has shown me how a real saint lives.

"Though I don't have a job, I would like to begin helping Mother Teresa in her work. All I have is what I get from my parents. So I'm going to give my 'allowance' which Mother Teresa's poor need a lot more than I do.

"I am grateful for having been made to think about those who, at my age, don't have half of what I do . . . ."

*Try to look for those who need you and try to get to know them personally. Do little things for them, those things which no one else has time to do.*

Mother Teresa

# from a scholar in France

Scientists and scholars pride themselves on their objectivity. But a certain modern French scholar has this to say: "Happiness is obvious in those who strive for a definite ideal. It makes all effort possible and enables them to overcome adversity. This is true of Mother Teresa who can serenely and sympathetically minister to lepers in their death houses. Try to endure for a few hours what her white-and-blue-sari-clad Sisters endure throughout their entire lives: extreme poverty, unbearable heat, offensive odors — all of which are so repugnant to people of refined tastes. Try, also, to be happy on only four spoonsful of rice for your daily sustenance. Then you will know that love is stronger than anything else. I believe that one is happy when one is consecrated to a cause.''

*Jesus can demand a great deal from us. It is precisely in those instances when he demands a great deal from us that we should give him a beautiful smile.*

Mother Teresa

## from a driver in a hurry

Wherever Missionaries of Charity live and work their schedules have one thing in common: They go to bed early and they get up very early. Father Hilario Rodríguez tells of a humorous incident that occurred when he was driving Mother Teresa to the Sisters' house in Catia la Mar, outside of Caracas.

They were returning from visiting the President of Venezuela; and it was 10:00 P.M., an extremely late hour for Mother Teresa. Father Rodríguez was consequently in a hurry, and a torrential rain had begun to fall.

The priest knew the road well and, at the outset, shared with Mother Teresa his anticipation of a later traffic jam. When, however, they reached the point where the traffic jam was supposed to be, he was pleasantly surprised. Expressing this to Mother Teresa, she offered her "explanation": God is very good.

However, she had no sooner spoken those words than the traffic became as heavy as predicted. Trying to contain his impatience, the priest chided her in jest, "Mother Teresa, you are wrong. God is not good." And Mother Teresa laughed at the ridiculousness of it all. He had seen her smile and laugh many times, but never quite like that night.

He kept on driving, thinking that at any moment he would be slowed down to crawling at a snail's pace with endless stoppings and startings until the wee hours of the morning. But the bottleneck never occurred, and the heavy traffic kept moving as if the road were nearly empty.

*We should not do our work with pride or vanity. Our work should be God's work. The poor are God's poor. Place yourselves under Jesus' influence in such a way that he can think his own thoughts in your mind, carry out his work through your hands. You will be able to do anything once his strength is yours.*

Mother Teresa

## from the author and his wife

The author was with Mother Teresa and the Sister who was to be the Superior of the new house in Leganés-Madrid at the bank when they opened an account. Mother Teresa used the occasion to show the Sister just how she should keep the account and manage the finances.

I noticed that not only did Mother Teresa make the sign of the cross before she signed the account but that, in general, her attitude was that of one who took money matters very, very seriously. I was later to learn why: Mother Teresa considers herself the administrator of sacred funds entrusted to her by the generosity of many — at the cost often of personal sacrifice. She respects such love and demands of herself and others that all live up to that trust.

*When suffering comes to you, welcome it with a smile. It is the greatest gift God can give you. Have the courage to accept anything God gives you with a smile and willingly give him anything he asks of you.*

Mother Teresa

# AND HER SMILE GOES ON REACHING OUT . . .

## to those open to new experiences

One of the most beautiful things about Mother Teresa's service to the poorest of the poor is that it is contagious. Symptoms of spontaneous generosity show up where least expected. Bricklayers and plumbers offer their services free of charge to build walls and fix sinks; students who have never done manual labor suddenly become apprentices and acquire their first blisters. A stewardess, used to serving whiskey or caviar to famous passengers on international flights, hurries, after having landed, to lovingly serve sandwiches and yogurt to orphans who live in a house staffed by the Missionaries of Charity.

When the first soup kitchen was established for the poor on a very old inner-city street in Madrid, Spain, it was in an area where there were quite a few bars, mediocre restaurants, and cheap boardinghouses.

Soon the young disco set became involved and virtually took over tearing down walls, removing debris, carrying bricks, and mixing mortar. As the work progressed, the people who lived along the street kept wondering what these young people were doing. They were very curious and sometimes asked, "What are they trying to do — build their own club or a disco?" But the young people kept their "secret," until finally the daily presence of Mother Teresa's Sisters made it clear to all what they were involved in.

One day a young lady, who had imbibed much more alcohol than she could handle, had to be almost literally carried to the place by her friends. But her fellow workers just drenched her with cold water, and she stayed to join in the work.

*Today, once more, Jesus comes among his own and his own do not know him. He comes in the hurt bodies of our poor. But he even comes in the rich who abound in riches. He comes in the loneliness of their hearts, when there is no one who loves them. Jesus comes to you and me. And often, very often, we let him pass without noticing him.*

Mother Teresa

## to those concerned about her work

Some people wondered out loud, "What will become of the work of the Missionaries of Charity after you die?"

And Mother Teresa's answer was, "Then I will look after it."

One of the coordinators voiced her concern to Mother Teresa in Oslo, "Perhaps it would be good to have an international meeting for all Co-Workers."

Mother Teresa raised her arms to heaven and said, "We are neither an organization nor a business!"

*My years of dedication and service to the poor have helped me to understand that it is precisely they who really understand human dignity. Their main problem is not their lack of money but the fact that their right to be treated humanly and lovingly is not recognized.*

Mother Teresa

## to those concerned about her Sisters

When Mother Teresa was about to open her first house in the Western hemisphere, in Cocorote, Venezuela, she and the Sisters were offered a very nice house with a refrigerator in it. Mother Teresa refused the house and the refrigerator, saying simply that the poor in Cocorote did not have such pretty houses nor refrigerators and her Sisters would not have them either.

Again, when the first house in Spain was being readied for the Sisters, her friends had accepted a washer and a refrigerator for the Sisters. How could they refuse such a generous offer? Her refusal to accept the refrigerator in Venezuela had taken place fourteen years earlier, in 1966, but in the 1980s even the poor have refrigerators.

When Mother Teresa saw the washer and the refrigerator, with delicacy she said, "The Sisters do not need the refrigerator or the washer."

Some argued with her that at some point the

Sisters might need to keep some medicine in a cold place, either for themselves or for others. Mother Teresa answered, "Fine. If they need one later on, God will provide. Right now they do not need it." (It so happened that two months later the Sisters opened a soup kitchen in Madrid, and the refrigerator was put to the service of the poor in accordance with Mother Teresa's wishes.)

Three days later, when Mother Teresa left, the author assured her, "Mother, don't worry, we will take very good care of the Sisters." To which she replied, "Help the Sisters to be poor!"

*****

Paul Charron, a Canadian Co-Worker of Mother Teresa, was present when the Missionaries of Charity opened a small house in Detroit in June 1979. He describes the event in one of the Co-Workers' publications.

"We had started with furnishing the house. But when the Sisters arrived, they asked us to remove the refrigerator which had been given to them. After breakfast, we welcomed Mother Teresa as well as two Sisters from India and one from the United States.

"When I saw Mother Teresa arrive with her coarse handbag, tied with a string, I was unable to stop my tears. It is impossible to describe her. She is one of God's marvels. She is living and tangible proof of God's love for us.

"At the meeting we had in the parish, Mother Teresa spoke about her work. Her message is always the same, but she added two phrases which really impressed me: 'My gift to you is my Sisters. Protect their poverty.' Then I understood having to take the refrigerator away.

"The simplicity and humility of Mother Teresa is always impressive. She radiates the indescribable inner happiness of Jesus' presence everywhere, from the moment of first contact."

*Christians are light for each other and for the rest of the world. If we are Christians we have to reveal Christ. Gandhi once said that if Christians truly lived their Christianity, there would be no Hindus in India. This, therefore, is what everyone expects from us: that our Christianity be real.*

Mother Teresa

## to those concerned about finances

Someone asked Mother Teresa whether she ever had money problems. She answered: "Money problems? Money doesn't worry me in the least. Money always comes. We do everything for the Lord, and he is the one who should worry about us. If he wants us to do something, it's up to him to grant us the means. If he doesn't, then that means he does not want us to carry out the work and we should give up trying."

*Ever since the very beginning of our Congregation, Catholic Relief Services has shared in, helped, and supported our work. The people of America have channeled, through that helpful organization, their donations which have made it possible for us to give food, clothing, and care to thousands and thousands of sick and needy people.*

Mother Teresa

# BUT MOTHER TERESA DOESN'T ALWAYS SMILE . . .

*That Mother Teresa's smile radiates the strength of Christ rather than weakness can be made clear from one last story:*

## the exploiters of the poor

After the opening of the first Missionaries of Charity house in Venezuela in 1966, a desperate need became known for a new center of hospitality for unwed mothers. The civil authorities also became aware of this, and the governor of the state of Vargas suggested to Mother Teresa that she look for a suitable location. The authorities assured her that, if the place and the price were right, they would take care of the finances. When a site was found, the lawyer who represented the owners of the land asked for a meeting of all involved.

According to my source, Mother Teresa went into the meeting with the assurance that she and the lawyer for the owners would reach agreement. Upon which she and the governor, who could not attend, would pay any price.

The lawyer announced the price would be 5,000,000 bolivars (something near one million dollars). At this, Mother Teresa threw her hands up in the air and expressed a very definite NO to the deal. And right after that, somewhat under her breath but with the same determination, she said: "You do not speculate with the poor!"

Obviously, there was no deal. The lawyer returned to his clients, taking Mother Teresa's NO with him. A few moments after that the governor arrived and asked Mother Teresa if an agreement had been reached. She said there was no agreement and explained why.

When she returned to the house located in Catia la Mar, Mother Teresa was still very upset, saying to those who were with her: "For God's sake! I cannot even imagine what would have happened if we had accepted such initial abuse at the expense of the poor."

*Today, nations put too much effort and money into defending their borders. They know very little about the poverty and the suffering which exist in the countries where those bordering on destitution live. If they would only defend these defenseless people with food, shelter, and clothing, I think the world would be a happier place.*

Mother Teresa

# APPENDIX

## Her Smile Beckons a Special Few
### *Paul Chetcuti, S.J.*

This appendix was originally published as a pamphlet under the title *Choosing to Serve the Destitute*. Liguori Publications is grateful to the copyright owner, Irish Messenger Publications, and the translator, Father Michael Paul Gallagher, S.J., for permission to reproduce it here.

I spent five months living and working in Calcutta with the Brothers and Sisters of Mother Teresa, and I should like to offer here some reflections inspired by this involvement, which was for me more than just an experience. One cannot have contact with human misery for months without it having an effect: to watch men and women die or struggle against death is more than an experience — it is to enter into something close to the core of human existence itself. It means having your deepest convictions called into question, being shaken in the innermost part of oneself; it is a kind of second baptism.

### Calcutta

It is not easy to describe what a person sees in Calcutta. The city seems to me like an open ulcer.

When you go there for the first time, you have the impression of arriving in a town that has just been bombed. Most of the houses are only half-constructions made from sheet metal, straw, and bamboo. All are held together in every imaginable way: cement, mud, rope, string, and so on.

The streets are congested to the utmost. Children in their thousands play or even relieve themselves along the footpath; whole families wash themselves at public pumps; little wooden boxes measuring only a few feet square serve as shops; cows cross, in unconcerned fashion, those same streets so full of traffic. In Calcutta people live more on the street than in the houses. Practically everything happens out of doors: playing, cooking, sleeping.

Then there are those for whom the street is their home because they cannot afford anything else. Thousands of villagers who come to make their living in Calcutta find that the rents are too high for them. There is only one solution: to set themselves up in the open air. It is cheaper. So they make a shelter by fastening some rags or large bits of plastic to a wall. That is their home. As for furniture, they make do with bricks, baskets, and scraps.

It is in such "lodgings" that thousands of people live and die. It is terrible to see these people when it rains during the night, staying awake, wet to the skin, waiting until the rain stops because their "tents" are in no way waterproof. At night, I have seen entire families shelter from the rain under a balcony, soaked to the bone —

parents, children, grandparents. Thousands of men and women have no other bed than the threshold of a house or the porch of some business premise. Those who have more luck find shelter in big drainage pipes that have been abandoned or else under a bridge. Bus stops and tram stops are the most sought after homes for these poor people because the roofs are made of concrete and do not leak.

## Selling Human Misery

To earn a living these unfortunates use every possible method: begging, rummaging, working, stealing. Everything is allowed. One must eat enough today to be able to face tomorrow. That is the only purpose of the day. Beggars are countless, and they make use of every imaginable handicap to capture the pity of the passerby. It is like a public sale of human misery. And it often happens that the worse the affliction is, the more lucrative the takings. I wanted to shout with rage one day when a leper approached me with his hands disfigured by the disease, proposing that I pay him to be allowed to take a photo of him. I gave him the money he asked, but I ran away as fast as possible, my camera heavy as lead on my shoulder.

What can one say about the thousands of people who make their living by searching systematically through the dustbins? In the piles of refuse that adorn the streets of Calcutta, they find old paper that they can sell for a few coins, or they come across some wood for their fire or half-burnt coal

which they wash as carefully as if it were gold —
then sell for what they can get. In Calcutta — it is
striking to find — that recycling of waste is both
spontaneous and highly effective. What one person throws away provides a living for someone
else. What cannot be eaten by man provides
nourishment for the thousands of cattle that make
their way through the streets of the city. Everything is used again; every empty jam jar is picked
up and used in countless ways. From all this we
rich people of the West could have much to learn.

## Sickness Is the End

As long as one is in good health, everything
goes fairly well. The worst time occurs when
anyone falls sick. For these people of the streets,
sickness is often the end, or very nearly so.
Doctors cost too much. So one has to look for help
in a State Clinic where treatment is free, at least in
theory; but in practice one can die before getting
any attention at all. These hospitals are so overcrowded that patients are placed anywhere and
everywhere — under the stairs, in corridors, in
every corner imaginable. A major problem for the
doctor is to prevent the admission of still more
patients. To cite one incident: two dying people
were admitted to the emergency ward only after
four hours of wrangling and haggling with the
doctor on duty. They had been picked up from the
footpaths and so were automatically forbidden
admission. They were too poor and had nobody to
"pull strings" for them; and in Calcutta, more
than perhaps anywhere else, you must have

"pull" to get anything done. Even after admission into a hospital, one has still to receive treatment. This can take time, and it sometimes happens that treatment only comes when it is far too late. Who is to blame? Little point in saying that the problems are complex. It is just impossible to look after the health of fourteen million citizens without the necessary equipment. Until such time as the facilities are available, it is the poor people who will continue to suffer. As far as the rich are concerned, I have seen in Calcutta clinics as well-equipped and as comfortable as any in Europe. Woe to those who have no means, for they will not survive!

To describe life in Calcutta, I find the word that sums it up best is "struggle." You have to fight for everything. Public transport is so crowded that more people travel on the outside of the buses and trams, hanging on to doors and windows, than one finds either sitting or standing inside. So it is quite a struggle to board a bus and again to get off; you have to struggle to book a place on a train, struggle to find a job or lodgings, struggle against the heat or against the monsoon downpour, struggle to get into a hospital, and struggle to scrape together the means for another day of miserable existence. The population problem of Calcutta is of frightening proportions.

## Deeper Meaning of Poverty
## — the Emptiness of Man

One could continue describing the sufferings of these people of Calcutta, both in spirit and in body, but it is important also to grasp the significance of this poverty. What struck me most, seeing these men and women walking the squalid streets, was how easy it is for man to lose his humanity. One of the Psalms says that God made man little less than a god, but I have seen men who were hardly better than beasts. Material poverty is not merely material; it is something that affects the whole of one's humanity. The hungry man can think of nothing besides food; his entire existence is centered on his bodily survival, and his spirit is destroyed. What caused me most pain, when helping these people worn out by hunger, was their eyes emptied of all expression or content. Poverty robs man of his humanity to such an extent that he becomes incapable of feeling even bitterness or anger: he is just empty. And this void is a terrible thing. It shows man shorn of his divine spark, no longer a temple of anything at all. It is truly Christ who is attacked, who descends into hell, when man is reduced to such a frightful solitude. Without spirit he is like someone without a center, and this lack leads him ultimately to a loss of meaning and an absence of God: this is hell.

The one thing which can still give hope is the fact that Christ descended into this hell. For our sake he took on himself the sins of humanity. Man can therefore retain his manhood, and need never completely lose his humanity because he who became man dwells within him, more intimately with him than a man may be to himself. It is here that salvation can be found.

# Missionaries of Charity
## in the Service
## of God and Man

This reality of the presence of Christ in man is indeed the touchstone of the Congregation of Mother Teresa. Her Sisters and Brothers are above all contemplatives in the service of this Presence in those most deprived of their humanity. They are servants who contemplate Christ in their neighbor and allow him to appear again among men. They discover Christ and make him manifest to others. They serve man not only for the sake of his humanity — which is what any social worker does — but for the sake of the divinity which expresses itself in his humanity. It is a service of such glory that it can be embodied in the humblest of realities. These men and women who consecrate themselves to God and to their brothers, following the charism of Mother Teresa, are simple and transparent people. They have only one qualification to do what they are doing: they love God and their neighbor. And the work they perform they keep doing "until it hurts," as Mother Teresa likes to say.

To love somebody means to suffer with him and for him. So, to take up the cause of the poor implies becoming poor as well. The Brothers and Sisters of Mother Teresa are all poor — their houses, their food, their life-style, everything about them is poor. Even at the intellectual and spiritual level, the Missionaries of Charity can be described as poor, most of them coming from poor villages, having had only a little education. There is little point in asking a Sister or Brother to explain the essentials of their vocation because they are unable to express this in words or concepts. Is this ignorance? To us Western intellectuals, it may seem so. But what allows them to live that life is neither eloquent expression nor precise articulation of any given topic; it is rather the fullness of the gift of themselves through love.

They are also poor spiritually, and quite frequently their spirituality has not reached any great stage of development. Certain basics, such as devotion to the blessed Eucharist, silent adoration, vocal prayer, the rosary, a powerful conviction that every poor man is none other than Christ, a desire to quench the thirst of Jesus — these are the pillars of their spiritual life. But when one tries to probe the meaning of these realities for their lives, one finds it difficult to see exactly how it all hangs together. Many of them cannot really appreciate the spiritual wealth contained in their own Constitutions. Quite often Brothers and Sisters, immediately after their novitiate, are sent to work in difficult places which do not always have a resident priest or spiritual director; so they have to find spiritual nourishment in the Gospels or in the text of their Constitutions. This lack of spiritual direction is a source of considerable distress to the Missionaries of Charity. What strikes you most in their spirituality is not so much its ''depth'' as its ''toughness''; it is a fairly traditional spirituality, satisfied with the bare essentials.

# By Their Fruits . . .

But a tree is judged by its fruits, and living with the Missionaries of Charity, one has the opportunity of sharing the fruits of this spirit: an overflowing joy, a deep faith, prayer. Joy is the sign which marks these men and women; like a balm, it envelops their communities and is contagious. It is the joy born from a total gift of oneself. If their life is hard, if poverty and love call them to die to themselves, at the same time they discover the springs of a peace that ''nothing can take away from them.'' Living with them, it is impossible not to feel your own heart on fire with a mysterious presence. This is the origin of a simple joy which the Missionaries of Charity spread around them in thousands of ways. This is how they sow love and cast out suffering. The great mystery of this joy lies in the fact that it can exist at all in situations of human misery and suffering which, in themselves, should arouse sadness and despair. How is it possible to remain joyful when surrounded by broken men and running sores, in the midst of groans and pain and even of the dead? One has to be either insensitive or a saint to be able to do so. The Missionaries of Charity are indeed saints.

They have a faith that moves mountains. It is easier to move the highest mountain than to love as they love. They are grounded in the charity that God is love and that he is actively present among us, among all men. For them that is enough. For God's power nothing is impossible, because what is impossible for man is possible for God. The Missionaries of Charity put their trust in this, and so achieve things that would be otherwise impossible.

## Total Trust in God

It is impossible to confront the problems of hunger in a city like Calcutta with only a handful of young men and girls of goodwill, without money and without know-how. But given that it is God who calls them, they tackle it with joy and with faith. They start by doing whatever they can, and God takes care of the rest. It does not matter if the man whom they are nursing resells the medicine that he gets from them. They give it to him with a prayer, and so God will be with this man much more than they can ever be. It does not greatly matter if they do not have the necessary vaccine for the treatment of this sick woman, because they give her what has been given to them free of charge — the love of God and the few medicines they possess. God will take care of this sick woman. To human eyes, this trust in God seems carried to excess, but it is the touchstone of the whole work of Mother Teresa. Her favorite saying is, "If God wants something, it will be done." This is how she can afford to make use only of "small means." She dares remain "small," even when faced with the enormity of the work. This weakness is her strength since it is the source of peace and serenity, where others might give up through discouragement and bitterness.

This unshakable faith finds its roots in deep and continuous prayer. For Mother Teresa everything begins there. It is prayer that puts a Brother or Sister in touch with God and makes them capable of being his instrument. It is through prayer that one learns to look contemplatively at the world and to discern there the living presence of Jesus. The Missionaries of Charity begin their day with prayer, both personal and communal, followed by the Eucharist which is the real center of their existence. Each evening they have an hour's adoration before the Blessed Sacrament. The Sisters have a rule of reciting the rosary when traveling or when walking through the streets. Everything is done in an atmosphere of prayer. I remember one occasion, while working in the home for the dying, when I went, in some agitation, to tell the Sister that a man was on the point of death. The first question she put to me was, ''Have you prayed for him?'' To pray is the first thing to be done, even before considering what is needed from a medical point of view. No wonder that their scale of values seems to challenge our more usual ones.

## The Eucharist —
## the Heart of the Work

In the life of the Missionaries of Charity more importance is given to prayer than to the actual work. ''We are not social workers,'' Mother Teresa will say, ''we are first and foremost contemplatives.'' And this contemplation starts with the Eucharist. It is because Christ really offers himself in the sacrifice of the Mass, and because he is really present in the Blessed Sacrament, that we can touch him in our brothers and sisters, in all mankind. Mother Teresa sees an intimate link between these two forms of the presence of Christ in our world, the first form being the source of the second. In fact she constantly holds up as a model to her Sisters the way in which the priest touches the Body of Christ at Mass: "This is how you should handle the same Body of Christ in the suffering bodies of men." It is indeed a Eucharistic vision of the world.

Beginning then from the Eucharist, as a sign of the powerful presence of the Risen Lord in our world, the work carried on by the Brothers and Sisters of Mother Teresa is one of adoration. Working with and for men means adoring him who became man so that men could share God's life. It means putting oneself at the service of the Incarnation of God in Jesus Christ and at the service of his Body as extending to all times and to all places. This identity between the Body of Christ — Eucharistic and mystical — and the body of man is the basis of all the work of the Missionaries of Charity. This is the real reason why they give themselves completely to tend the body of man, even in its most ravaged state; it is these same bodies, these same arms, these same emaciated legs, this same chest almost lacking the power to breathe, this same spent look, all of these form the throne of the majesty of God. They believe and they understand clearly why Jesus was truly man, flesh of our flesh, blood of our blood, and this same Jesus is still alive today.

To serve man entails taking human history seriously as God himself has done, to the point where our history and his merge into a unity. With the coming of Jesus, this union was realized in its fullness. To take seriously the life story of each individual man, as Jesus did, means a letting go of all control over self and over others. It means putting oneself unreservedly in an attitude of receptiveness toward God who gives himself through the life story of each individual person.

The vocation of the Missionaries of Charity is focused on giving a welcome to the stranger and doing so in a way that is free, unconditional, and total. Such a welcome presupposes the acceptance of the other person as he or she is. This is, in fact, what is striking in the homes of Mother Teresa: Everybody is welcome. Nothing is asked of the guest or of the sick, not even the certainty that he or she will actually benefit from any help given. It is remarkable to see the readiness with which the Missionaries of Charity receive the same invalids over and over again; once recovered from their illness, they go back to the streets and, after a time, inevitably come back to the Sisters in a state often worse than before. The Sisters always receive them and start all over again. It is characteristic of the very poorest that they can never be finally "discharged." To Western eyes it simply does not make sense to act like this with hopeless cases. The Missionaries of Charity do not believe that anybody is beyond recovery; every case, even the most desperate, contains a hidden promise. Thanks to Christ, alive today, every life story is one of promise.

## Is Mother Teresa's Work Really Effective?

There are many who might reproach Mother Teresa with offering nothing except a short-term softening of the vast problems that beset the world; she solves none of them. But to understand her mission better, at this level, it is necessary to bear certain aspects of her work in mind. For her, what comes first is not the problem to be solved but, rather, the person affected. Such an attitude is deeply evangelical. Her charism consists in personalizing reality, while more often than not we tend to theorize about a reality under the pretext of taking a more global approach to it. She never asks what should be done, but what I, you, he, or she can do. To take the history of men seriously is to make oneself vulnerable to them. Moreover, the efficacy of Mother Teresa's work cannot be measured by the success, direct or indirect, of what is achieved by the Brothers and Sisters. Sociologically, public opinion is one of the most powerful factors for changing social structures — and it is on this level that the *causes* of all injustices and human suffering should be located. It can moreover be claimed without any hesitation that very few people have mobilized public opinion so strongly as has Mother. Thanks to her and to the publicity she receives — even against her own wishes — the poor are more known, more loved, better defended, even if sometimes this publicity is out of all proportion to what Mother Teresa actually achieves in a concrete way. Almost single-handedly, this little woman has awakened a new conscience among thousands of people, and this alerting of conscience, so urgently needed, can and should become effective in changing the unjust structures of our societies. So, even from the viewpoint of human effectiveness, Mother Teresa's work has a considerable impact. But with regard to those who still criticize her work: Insofar as they do so as external observers, they cannot possibly appreciate its real value for those who benefit from it. It is only through my work in the hospices for the dying that I could glimpse the all-powerful love that is the beginning and end of this work.

The poorest of all are those who have been deprived even of their humanity. To be hungry is to be enslaved within one's biological needs, limited to an existence whose horizons shrink to the piece of bread one wants or the bowl of rice one longs for. Poverty of this kind is like the withering or burial of one's humanity. But if one works out of love for these outcasts, one can sometimes witness the most marvelous miracle. It makes one feel like dancing for joy to find one day that a man, wasted away by hunger and disease, asks to have his nails cut or to have his beard trimmed to his liking or for a clean shirt. Such a man is saved; he has recovered the sense of what is beautiful and of what is right. He has risen from the purely biological level of existence to the aesthetic, from necessities of life to some of life's freedoms. He has become man again. Only the victory of love could have brought about this re-creation of him, allowing him to rediscover his humanity. In this way love unveils the image of God in men and women whom hardship had reduced to nothing.

Faced with such a reality one no longer speaks of efficacy or inefficacy. One chooses, rather, silence and adoration. One worships before the mystery of life, of love, and of suffering for which no price is too low or too high. For each of these men and women the ultimate price was the precious blood of our Lord Jesus Christ, and it is through associating themselves with this redemptive suffering that the Brothers and Sisters can live from a profound compassion for the sufferings of men, their brothers in the same Christ. Just as Jesus was offered up for us, so his Spirit exorcises suffering and transforms it into a source of life. Man can live because God has taken upon himself both pain and death. "There is no greater love than to lay down one's life for one's friends," to serve men for the sake of Christ means dying with him so that they may live.

## The Option for
## the Most Humble

To die with Christ does not only mean accepting gladly all that is humble or insignificant but seeking it out deliberately. This is why Mother Teresa has made a basic choice in favor of the weakest. In her way of life and her actions she poses a fundamental question to all human power.

Of small stature herself, she demands that her Brothers and Sisters should be, in another sense, "small people" working for the least of the poor, with only humble means. This littleness is shown also in the way in which she trains her Missionaries of Charity. No great plans inspire the formation of these young men and women who wish to give their all. Some classes on medicine are given when there is a doctor who offers his services. A Brother, whose work for years among lepers has taught him all there is to know about the disease, lectures to those assigned to this work. One or two of the Sisters happen to be doctors, but no effort is made to send others for medical studies.

On the spiritual side also, there are only two priests to look after the needs of the motherhouse in Calcutta, where some three hundred Sisters receive their formation. Is this a weakness? In our view it is a serious one. But the question necessarily arises: Must not "being small" and therefore weak (in a real and not just superficial way) cause pain and make one vulnerable? In the most intimate center of their being, on the spiritual and professional level, these souls fired with love remain weak and small.

Likewise, by their own deliberate choice they use only the most humble means in their work. Mother Teresa refuses, on principle, to make any of her works of charity into an institution. For example, she refuses to have hospitals. In her home for the dying in Calcutta she refuses to employ a full-time doctor, and is happy simply to have the free service of one or two doctors who volunteer their time. She refuses all sophisticated equipment in her homes, even a simple microscope which could be useful for the rapid diagnosis of certain sicknesses. In her eyes this would be the first step toward the establishment of an institution for sick people. And before long the institution could become more important than the patients.

Besides, institutions tend to establish themselves at the expense of those who are poorest. By definition, it would seem, an institution must devote itself to helping the invalid or the poor man in ways that are effective for the long term. If an institution is working along normal medical lines, this will mean giving priority and the best treatment to those with the best chances of recovery and of being discharged. An institution will cut short or even refuse treatment to incurable cases, and this in turn entails a selection of patients. Only those with some hope of improvement will be accepted for treatment, if for no other reason than availability of beds. This means that those with no hope of recovery, those who are dying, find themselves refused admission into those institutions which were originally intended for them.

No, the doors must always be open to those who are truly the smallest and poorest of people. To set up an institution might possibly serve the poor but not necessarily the poorest of the poor. But Mother Teresa's vocation is precisely this, and she is fiercely loyal to it. Anyone who does not grasp this point will probably be shocked at the merely rudimentary level of treatment available in the homes of Mother Teresa. Incompetence is not at all excluded; mistakes are made. But this is the only way to remain "small" and thus genuinely at the service of the least of men.

This is a difficult situation to come to terms with, and our pride tends to react against it. We would want to be efficient, to be able to follow up those who leave a home after a stay of two or three months and who go back to the streets homeless, without money, with only a little more strength than they had when they were brought to it. But it is at this price that one says "yes" to God, thus proving that the work which we achieve is not all our own doing. You are thoroughly poor when you do not even gather the fruits of your efforts on the level of effectiveness. It is like sacrificing "the only son, the bearer of the promise," as did Abraham, our father in faith. This is obedience in faith and the only source of spiritual fruitfulness. It bears witness to the fact that God alone can save: We are only his "useless servants."

## Mother Teresa as
## Prophet for Our Times

In this challenging way Mother Teresa is truly a prophet for our times. It is her charism to proclaim in our Church and in our godless world that only God saves with gentleness, with patience, humbly, by becoming, in Jesus our Redeemer, the least among men. At a time of unprecedented talk about poverty, often in a context of unprecedented material well-being, and at a time when thousands of gods offer themselves as man's salvation — by means of financial, technical, or ideological power — Mother Teresa proclaims in her frail and small voice that the only way to salvation is the way of weakness, of insignificance, of serving men in him who is the sole master and servant of all. She teaches us to be patient with the patience of God himself, who walks our roads with human footsteps. It is he who renews the universe because he "has so loved the world that he sent his only Son so that he who believes may have eternal life."

Only if we die with the Son can the life of the Father take us over, and this life will change our world into a kingdom of true freedom, of real salvation, because this life is spirit and it is love. May God allow us to bear witness to this in our own time and place, even "until it hurts," for "we know in effect that all creation even to this day groans under the pains of childbirth." More than that: "We ourselves who possess the first fruits of the Spirit, groan in our hearts in the expectation of the redemption of our body. Because our salvation is founded on hope" (Romans 8:19-24).

# OTHER HELPFUL BOOKS FROM LIGUORI

## Jesus' Pattern for a Happy Life: THE BEATITUDES
### by Marilyn Norquist Gustin

This beautiful, joy-filled book invites you to dismiss the idea that the Beatitudes are a set of rules only a saint could follow and to consider the Beatitudes as a pattern for peace — a plan that *can* be followed in today's world. The author asks you to follow this pattern and discover the meaning of "blessedness" on this earth, in your life, and in your world. **$3.50**

## DARE TO BE CHRISTIAN
### Developing a Social Conscience
### by Bernard Häring, C.SS.R.

This book may well change your whole idea of "holiness." In this book, Bernard Häring's idea of a saint is not a killjoy with a sour face or someone who sits in a corner and withdraws from the world to work on private "holiness." Instead, he sees the "saint," the true Christian, as one who follows the example of Christ and reaches out to others — to be "light to the world." **$4.25**

## INNER CALM
### by Dr. Paul DeBlassie, III

In today's hurried, harried world, we all long for a greater sense of peace and joy, a true inner calm. This book addresses that need and explains the beauty and hope of the "Jesus Prayer." In this "Christian answer to modern stress," the author shares with the reader a wealth of healing experiences and offers an invitation to discover the true meaning of inner calm in today's world. **$3.95**

## HOW TO FORGIVE YOURSELF AND OTHERS
### Steps to Reconciliation
#### *by Reverend Eamon Tobin*

It's something hard to forgive others — but even harder to forgive yourself. This book shows how to let go of deep hurts, mend broken relationships, and learn about forgiving. Presenting a simple yet effective plan for personal and interpersonal healing, it offers hope and reassurance to anyone who sincerely seeks reconciliation. **$1.50**

## "THY KINGDOM COME . . .
### The Basic Teachings of Jesus
#### *by Marilyn Norquist Gustin*

Jesus never stopped urging his hearers to live in the Kingdom. Yet he never said exactly what it is — he only told what it "is like" — because the Kingdom of God is not an idea to be analyzed but a reality to be lived.

How do you begin to live in the Kingdom? This is what this book will help you discover. Each of its seventeen chapters explains Jesus' message about the Kingdom and provides guidelines for prayerful reflection, discussion, and practical action.

If you seek the Kingdom of God, this book will help you to discover it, experience it, and live it! **$1.50**

## THE SINGLE LIFE
### A Christian Challenge
#### *by Martha M. Niemann*

A book for those faced with the ups and downs, joys and sorrows, hopes and frustrations of being a single Christian adult. Thirty brief chapters explore the unique problems and situations of single life and help readers discover the roads to happiness as single Christians. **$4.25**

### · HOW YOU CAN BE A PEACEMAKER
### Catholic Teachings and Practical Suggestions
#### by Mary Evelyn Jegen, SND

A helpful handbook that combines spiritual wisdom and workable suggestions for individuals and groups. Part One discusses basic teachings on peace — those of Jesus, Pope John Paul II, and the U.S. bishops. Part Two focuses on our role as teachers and models of peace and suggests ways to extend peacemaking locally and globally. Includes questions for discussion and an index. **$2.95**

### THE BIBLE, THE CHURCH, AND SOCIAL JUSTICE
#### by Richard Schiblin, C.SS.R.

This thought-provoking book takes a careful look at the controversial issue of social justice as it applies to today's world. The author draws from his own experience and from other sources to give readers a clearer understanding of the meaning of social justice and an explanation of both the Bible's and the Church's position on the subject. This is a book for the ''average Christian'' who is concerned — or should be — about issues of injustice, poverty, and oppression. A particularly helpful aspect of this book is that it presents practical steps that the ''average Christian'' can take to bring about social change. **$1.50**

Order from your local bookstore or write to:
**Liguori Publications,** Box 060, Liguori, Missouri 63057
*(Please add 75¢ for postage and handling for
first item ordered and 25¢ for each additional item.)*